Across the Rainbow Bridge

Published by Glorybound Publishing
SAN 256-4564
10 9 8 7 6 5 4 3 2 1
Printed in the United States of America
KDP ISBN 9781699673898
Copyright Data available on file.
Burton, Gorden, 1951-
        Across the Rainbow Bridge/G.W. Burton
        Includes biographical reference.
1. Inspirational Book   2. Book on Dogs
I. Title

www.gloryboundpublishing.com

On the Cover:
Chyna, my dog from 2008 to 2012. She was a greyhound dalmation mix. She was the dog that chose us! The flower bed was her favorite place to rest. It seems an appropriate picture for the cover since she has passed on to a better place.

Across the Rainbow Bridge

By
G.W. Burton

Glorybound Publishing
Camp Verde, Arizona
Released 2019

Letter from the Author

Dear Reader,

I already know you have and love dogs or you wouldn't even be reading this. I also know that you have lost dogs, have had beloved canine companions who have crossed the Rainbow Bridge. You know the pain this has brought into your life, but you know as well the joy that only dogs can bring.

Thank you for your love and care for these marvelously faithful and loyal creatures. While it is true that God created all animals, ourselves included, I believe there is a special place in God's kingdom for dogs.

Is it any wonder that "God" is "dog" spelled backwards.

Thank you also for having enough interest in the dogs who have made my life so much better for their being in it. In these pages I hope you will find glimpses of your dogs, and that these stories will make you smile, or cry, but most of all remember.

Thank you, and God/dog bless you,

Gordon W. Burton

TESTIMONIAL

I must confess that Gordon, the author, is my husband, so my words are not without bias.

In addition, I have known well most of the dogs chronicled here, and Gordon has told me stories of the rest.

Still, as I read these page, I found myself crying once in a while, laughing even more, but more often fondly remembering each of these loving creatures.

This book helps keep their memories alive for me, and for that I am grateful.

Cami Pollard-Burton

The Rainbow Bridge

Just this side of heaven is a place called Rainbow Bridge.

When an animal dies that has been especially close to someone here, that pet goes to Rainbow Bridge. There are meadows and hills for all of our special friends so they can run and play together. There is plenty of food, water and sunshine, and our friends are warm and comfortable.

All the animals who had been ill and old are restored to health and vigor. Those who were hurt or maimed are made whole and strong again, just as we remember them in our dreams of days and times gone by. The animals are happy and content, except for one small thing; they each miss someone very special to them, who had to be left behind.

They all run and play together, but the day comes when one suddenly stops and looks into the distance. His bright eyes are intent. His eager body quivers. Suddenly he begins to run from the group, flying over the green grass, his legs carrying him faster and faster.

You have been spotted, and when you and your special friend finally meet, you cling together in joyous reunion, never to be parted again. The happy kisses rain upon your face; your hands again caress the beloved head, and you look once more into the trusting eyes of your pet, so long gone from your life but never absent from your heart.

Then you cross Rainbow Bridge together....

Author unknown... *RainbowBridge.com*

INTRODUCTION

There are those who are not sure this poem means what we think it does, but that does not matter. There is comfort in the thought that our dogs, who were old and sick, or young and ill, or injured beyond veterinary science ability to overcome have gone from this place to a better one. And that they have gone to a place where we will one day see them again. As someone said, "heaven is the place where all the dogs you have ever loved come to greet you." That is the place beyond the Rainbow Bridge.

The pages which follow are about those dogs I hope will be waiting for me on the other side of that bridge. In my words, people who have had dogs as beloved family members will probably not read anything they haven't known or thought or felt. If there are new thoughts and insights, that is all the better. If all this does is to help you remember your canine companions, then I am satisfied.

This book is not intended to be a DIY for dog people, a " how-to" on raising and living with dogs and finally being able to let them go. It is simply an account of my lives with dogs "warts and all", as they say. I have cared well for them, we have made some mistakes with them. My experience is that they have loved me through it all, and for that I am grateful and blessed.

For me, these chapters make up the whole of my life to date with dogs. There was a large hiatus in between the early canine companions and those who came much later in my life. There was a time when I had no dogs. I didn't realize how my life was diminished until later dogs were brought back into my life. I can reliably say there will never again be a time when there is not at least one dog, quite probably more in my home and my heart.

In what follows, I will simply tell you about my beloved dogs, without commentary as to what, if anything they taught me. I know my life has been greatly enriched by their lives. These lives speak for themselves quite well. The writing of this book has been a walk down memory lane. As you, the reader, takes this walk with me, I hope this shared walk will bring to your mind the memories of your departed canine companions.

Proverbs 10:7 says it perhaps best: "The memory of the righteous is a blessing." May I be forgiven if I claim to much, but to me all my dogs deserve to be seen and remembered as righteous, for their memories are indeed blessings to me.

LADY

Lady was the one who introduced me to the love of dogs. Lady was a small, female beagle my parents thought would be good for me. She was, though to be honest, I do not have much of an active memory of Lady. I was six years old when Lady came to live with us. What I know of her has come from old black and white photos and the stories my mother told me about her while we were looking at those photos.

My primary memory of Lady is of her death. We lived in a small town in Northern Indiana, the kind of town where people did not lock their doors at night, where it was common to leave the car keys on the dashboard, so they were always there. It was a town where children roamed the streets playing unafraid of any "stranger danger." It was a town where everyone knew everyone else and knew everyone else's business. It was a town where news of my misbehavior and discipline at school made it home before I did. It was a town where dogs were not leashed or tied out. They, like we, were free to roam.

Lady was not one to chase cars. Our yard was not large, but there was room to play and play in it she did; until the day came when she didn't. Until the day she, for whatever reason, chose to chase the milkman, and came under the wheels of his truck. He was disconsolate, as was my mother. I was at school when this happened. Lady's body had been taken away even before I was told that my dog had run after a truck, got hit, and was killed. My first pet also became my first lesson in life and death.

SHAMUS

It was a couple of years before we had another dog, and I don't truly remember the circumstances of how Shamus became a part of our family.

Shamus was an older dog, a bloodhound mix, complete with a long snout and droopy ears. He was a boy-dog, and I was old enough to associate bloodhounds with detectives, and Shamus was the nickname of every detective, so my bloodhound became Shamus.

Like a lot of bloodhounds, Shamus was not the most energetic of dogs. In fact, my memory of Shamus is that of being lazy. I was old enough to be involved in activities at school and around town, so my time spent with Shamus was not nearly as much as with Lady, though it was Shamus who began to teach me that time with a dog need not always be running and playing. Sitting in his presence was a time to be treasured.

Shamus suffered the same fate as Lady, with one important difference. He, too, decided to chase a vehicle, but it didn't kill him. It only left him lame, damaging one of his hind legs so that instead of walking or running, he would pull himself around by his front legs, dragging his backside behind him.

People might think it would have been more appropriate to have this animal put down, but it never crossed our minds. What we did, instead, was to move Shamus from our house in town to my grandparent's farm, where he could run, or drag himself around with the other farm dogs, which he did for many years before he died quietly of old age.

KING

King was not my dog, but I grew to think
of him in that way. King was an aging blind
German Shephard living with my Aunt Ruby
and Uncle Walter. Aunt Ruby was one of my
grandmother's sisters, and she and Uncle Walter
lived not far out of town. King was no longer
able to run loose, so he was tethered to his dog
house in the shade of a tree by the house. He
knew people were there by sound and scent, and
I like to think he knew me. At any rate, much of
my time with my Aunt and Uncle was spent by
King's house just sitting in the shade and petting
him. The lesson in quiet time which had started
with Shamus continued with King.

King died, like Shamus, of old age, and shortly
thereafter Aunt Ruby and Uncle Walter sold their
house in the country and moved into town. They
never had another dog.

ENGLISH SETTER

When Shamus moved to the farm, we did not immediately get another dog. I was able to see Shamus there and King at my Aunt and Uncles, and this seemed to satisfy the need for canine companionship.

I am not sure when we welcomed the English Setter into our home, nor do I even remember his name, for he did not live with us long. I know he was young and extremely active. I was in high school and also very active. My brothers, both younger, and I were not able to adequately for or give this wonderfully playful dog the time he needed. One day, while in the yard alone, he decided he needed to shred the laundry hanging on the clothesline. Needless to say, that did not go over well. Soon this boy was re-homed to a local farmer who had both time and space to care for this spirited creature properly. What I remember was he was white with brown spots, and always happy, jumping and running almost constantly, which was a joy to behold.

BUDDY

Buddy was not my dog, either. He had been a Christmas surprise for my youngest brother, Gene. Buddy was a Schipperke, only the second of that breed we had come to know. The first, Teddy, had been the camp dog of the fishing camp in Northern Minnesota went to every summer for many years

Because of Teddy, Buddy came into our lives. Buddy really belonged to all of us and had personality plus. True to his breed, he was an avid hunter of mice and any other small critters he could find. When he was not home, it was not unusual to find him in the barnyard across the street hunting mice and even rats in the barn and corn crib. The neighbor/farmer loved Buddy.

One vivid memory of Buddy is that he was a gregarious little guy, taking to almost everyone who came to the house. Almost. He didn't like our pastor, for whatever reason, and seemed to know when it was the pastor at the door. For him only would Buddy charge the door barking like a mad dog and jumping up to look out the window of the door, some five feet off the floor. The pastor would not come in until Buddy was contained. To my knowledge, we never figured out this behavior.

I have no active memory of Buddy's last days or his death, as I had gone to college by that time. I do remember him, Teddy, and to this day have a great affection for the Schipperke, as does almost everyone in the family. My little brother, now retired, has another Schipperke, Pete, who is like an elderly Buddy.

HANS

Then there was Hans. Hans was a mischievous little dachshund my uncle had given my grandparents. Hans was the first house dog my grandparents ever had on the farm, and Hans could get away with anything and everything that we grandchildren could not. My fondest memory of Hans is when he would beg; he would rise up, his front legs in the air, and rest on his butt waiting to be treated, not changing this posture until the treat was well in mouth.

Hans lived many years, and only crossed the bridge much later after I had children. He was failing, and my grandparents were struggling with when to have Hans put to sleep. Hans made it easier for them by going to sleep and crossing the bridge that night.

Hans was the first dog my son and daughter were close to, and his crossing brought many tears to their eyes.

BRUTUS

After seminary, I went to be the associate
pastor at an urban congregation. We lived in a
church-owned house and had a large yard. We
did not talk of getting a dog, but Brutus came
briefly into our care.

Brutus had been the dog of a local police
officer who was a member of my church. He
had recently acquired this majestic Doberman
Pincher. He was also going through a divorce
and could no longer care for King. I told him I
could not afford to buy Brutus, only to be told he
was not for sale, only needing a new home.

So shortly before the birth of our second child,
Brutus came to live with us. He was less than a
year old, energetic, and loyal.

One day I was in the yard pushing our son
on a swing. Brutus was roaming the back

fence. I was called to the front of the house by a neighbor, and when I came back to the yard, Brutus was slowly walking circles around the swing set, much to my son's delight. It was clear no one was going to get anywhere near that little boy without going through Brutus first.

For all his menacing looks, Brutus was a bit of a fraidy-cat, which is unusual for a big dog. I learned this one evening when walking him down the street, a neighbor's door was open, and two little toy poodles came charging out the door barking up a storm. The next thing I knew Brutus, this 65 pound Doberman, was cowering behind me, clearly wanting me to protect him from these ferocious beasts.

Sadly we were unable to keep Brutus. Our daughter was born, and a high energy dog with a newborn did not work. We re-homed him to my parents, who were also unable to keep him, due to an upcoming move to a new town. We all felt guilty over shuffling this marvelous dog from place to place.

Brutus' saga does have a happy ending. My parents contacted his breeder, who was more than willing to take him back. It seemed the breeder was working with a young girl who wanted to work with dogs in 4-H. She was caring for dogs at the breeders because she could not afford a dog of her own. Brutus became her dog, and we were told both dog and girl were thrilled and worked well together.

After this, I lost track of Brutus, and can only surmise that he is no longer living. My memory of him is of a noble beast with a loving and caring heart.

Mollie

MOLLIE & MYLES

After a long hiatus, my life with dogs began again with the marriage to my wife and soulmate, Cami. She brought two dogs into my life with her. Mollie was an aging Boston Terrier, and Myles a Cairn Terrier one year younger than Mollie. Myles was the spitting image of Toto, from The Wizard of Oz, and with him began Cami's love of all things OZ, especially all things Toto. When Myles came into Mollie's life, these two dogs had never been separated. When Cami and her husband divorced, Cami retained custody of Mollie and Myles.

I must confess that I was apprehensive about Mollie and Myles, or rather how they would respond to me. I knew for a fact, beyond any shadow of any doubt at all that if they did not like me, any chance I had of a further relationship with Cami was over. She later confirmed this fact for me.

Short answer, I was accepted. These two little dogs welcomed me into their family and were soon finding my lap in the evening, running to me when I came home from work. Of course, it didn't hurt that I was often the one to feed them.

For a while, we were a family of four. Mollie and Myles adjusted to the new house Cami had moved into with them, and they took me into the house as well when we married. There was a large, fenced yard to play in, front and back, plenty of squirrels to chase. One of our treasured photos is of the two of them having treed a squirrel in the Rose of Sharon tree in the backyard. They were happy dogs, loving to cuddle. They inaugurated a morning routine that we follow to this day. The morning begins in bed, with coffee and the news, the dogs cuddled around us. Another favored photo is Myles burying his nose in Cami's morning coffee, laced with Irish Cream. Beginning the morning with canine cuddles has become an important ritual which we follow to this day.

The only cloud on the horizon was that Mollie

had epilepsy and was on strong medication to help control the seizures. I will never forget when I experienced her first seizure, which was terrifying for me, and I can only imagine how much more so it was for her. Mollie began to show us signs that the end of her life was near. Not only were her seizures becoming more frequent, but she was also showing signs of dementia. Before we had the talk with the veterinarian, we wanted to be sure Myles would be all right. He had never been without a canine companion. Our thought was to adopt another small dog, enlarge the family so that Mollie's leaving would not be so traumatic for Myles.

This is when Chyna came into the family, and her story follows, so you will have to wait to learn more about her.

Suffice it to say; life did not go as we had thought or planned. When Chyna was introduced into the household, we thought Mollie would decline more rapidly, only to have her rally and live many more months. So we were a family of five for a while.

Mollie eventually succumbed to her conditions and crossed the bridge peacefully at the vet's office with Myles by her side. Chyna was waiting at home when we arrived. There were signs of the sadness of grief in both Myles and Chyna, but they had each other and us. We all cried for Mollie in our own way.

TEARS FOR MOLLY

Today I cried
tears for Molly,
for what I hope
she doesn't understand
and what I pray
she does.
I hope her cooked little brain
does not
cannot know
the ravages of time
and disease
on her tired
old
body.
Please
dear God of all earth's creatures
let that be beyond
her understanding,
would that it were beyond ours.
Just so I pray
she does know

how much
how very much
she is loved.
Little dog,
smallest of our pack,
yet Alpha all the same,
never shy to let the others know.
First to find an empty lap
and settle in
never the last
for a treat.
I pray she somehow knows
how much
she will be missed,
the weight of a dog
on a lap
is never too heavy,
she was never was,
nor will be so heavy
as when she is gone.

October 10, 2010

Myles was the next to go. For a while he and Chyna were our only dogs, then along came Rxby and Olive. (Their stories are to come). Myles was a Cairn Terrier, the runt of a litter who came into Cami's household a year after Mollie did. He had never been without a canine companion.

Myles had been weaned on beer and remained a boozehound all his days. He would lap beer up from the ground and then look up for more with a little Elvis grin. He loved to bury his head in his mommy's coffee when she had laced it with Irish Crème. Hence the picture of him with his head buried in her "don't make me call the flying monkeys mug" from Wicked, which was even more appropriate as Myles was Toto to a T.

*Disclaimer: We do know that alcohol is not especially good for dogs. In our defense, Myles was weaned before he came into Cami's home, without her knowledge or consent. This is not anything we would have done, but it was done, and doesn't seem to have harmed Myles, loveable little guy that he was.

Myles was a superb judge of character, and I was so relieved when I passed muster. If he liked a person, that person was trustworthy, and Myles liked most people he met. However, there was one incident when a friend brought her new boyfriend over to the house before we were all to go out. Our friend and her date came into the house, Myles loved our friend and was trotting toward her when he suddenly stopped and stood behind us, growling at the man beside her. We thought this odd. Several weeks later, our friend told us she had broken it off as the man was a terribly abusive person. Myles had known from the very first time he laid eyes on him.

Myles had also started to deteriorate with age, having hip problems. He would sometimes almost drag his back legs. We bought him a wheelchair to use at those times. It was almost comical to see him tooling around in his "chair", front legs running, hindquarters following on wheels.

For Myles the end was sudden and unpleasant. I would always get home from work first and would be greeted at the back door by all the dogs, for I would be the one to feed them. One day the other three, Rxby Chyna and Olive came to the door, standing at the top of the back stairs and just stood there. No Myles. I found him in the backroom, lying on the floor, unable to move but clearly alive and in great distress. I called to him, and he looked at me, making no attempt to move. I sat beside him and pulled him onto my lap, wrapping him in a soft towel. He had lost bowel control at some point, but there was no way to clean him, so we just sat there on the floor of the back room. I called Cami and left a message for her to call me as soon as she was out of session (she always left her phone off but voice mail on.) Myles and I sat, the other three watching us, occasionally coming to sniff and nuzzle him.

Cami called as soon as she picked up my message and came home immediately. I half expected Myles to die in her arms, but he was struggling to hang on. We decided it was time; this little trooper was to suffer no more. Wrapped in the towel, we carried him to the car, not before making sure the neighbor children

who very much loved Myles were back in their
house. The emergency vet was gracious and kind,
and Myles died in our arms that night. There
has never been a dog quite like Myles, and likely
never will be.

CHYNA

Chyna, a Greyhound/Dalmatian mix, was adopted from the local Humane Society to be a companion to Myles when Mollie died. We went to the Humane Society looking for another smaller dog, not necessarily a given breed, but small, about Myles size, which was 15-18 pounds.

Walking through the kennel area, we spotted Chyna, a larger black mixed-breed, laying in the rear of her kennel. As we approached, she rose and came to the door, poking her nose through the fence. The attendant told us that Chyna knew it was time for a walk, but due to an adoption event, they did not have the staff to attend to this. We said we could walk her a bit.

She came outside with us with absolutely no hesitation, and we strolled the yard for a while. She never left our side, and it was decided before the walk was over that this was a dog we could adopt, regardless of her larger size. We talked, walked, cussed, and discussed and made the decision. We wanted Chyna. The attendant we spoke with was thrilled and asked us to bring Chyna back to her kennel so we could go into the lobby and begin the paperwork to take her into our family.

Chyna had other ideas. As we approached the door of her kennel, she lagged behind us and finally came to a complete stop. She locked all four legs and refused to go any further. The only way to get her back into the kennel was to pick her up and carry her, all 55 pounds of her, or to drag her across the concrete floor, neither of which we were going to do. The attendant informed us that she would not be able to be in the lobby with us, there would be too much commotion and she might react to all the other people and dogs. Chyna still had nothing to do with the kennel. So we took her out to the lobby with us anyway. Chyna gave lie to the concerns of the attendant, sitting quietly between us as we did what we needed to do. It was clear that though we might have chosen Chyna, she had chosen us first.

Chyna was a cat-killer. At least that is what we were told by the Humane society as the reason she had been returned to them not once but twice. She had attempted to kill the family cats. So she could not be adopted to a household with cats. While we had smaller dogs, we had no cats. Chyna came home, and with a little socializing, she fit right in and became the third, as we anticipated Mollie's passing, which did not happen for some time.

At first, Chyna was a little nippy, would wait until another animal had walked by, then nip at their behind. We addressed this by the use of a soft muzzle, which we put on her when introducing her to a new animal. The muzzle was a signal that this new creature was to be accepted and not attacked. This worked very well, even when we introduced a cat into the household. Ghost came to us from Cami's son. She was a Snowshoe, and eventually, she and Chyna would cuddle and sleep together. So much for being a cat-killer.

In addition to the soft muzzle, we did introduce Chyna to a neighbor's dog, a Great Dane, albeit a small one. Miss Charlotte was only about 120 pounds. Chyna was 55. We thought it might be a good idea for Chyna to meet someone larger than herself. We sat on the patio of Miss Charlotte's home with her parents. All went well for a while. Then Chyna, true to form, waited until Miss Charlotte had passed by and nipped at her behind. Miss Charlotte stopped, slowly turned her head without making a sound, and made eye contact with Chyna. Chyna suddenly turned and bolted to the other side of the yard. For the rest of the evening, Chyna would not go anywhere near Miss Charlotte. Chyna also stopped nipping at anyone else.

Chyna was a sweet dog. The only small creatures she did go after were squirrels, and this ended the day she got hold of one, and it got hold of her by the ear. From that day forward, she showed no interest in chasing anything.

Chyna was storm shy. She was our weather-forecaster. Before a storm would roll in, she would get antsy, would get clingy, would jump up into the nearest lap and hide. She did not like thunder and lightning, leading us to the thought that she had been left out in storms at one time or another.

   She had a mischievous side as well, which got her into trouble. One Valentine's Day I had purchased special dark M&M's for Cami. We went out and when we came home found the bag, empty, on the floor, and chocolate on Chyna's gums. She had gotten on the table and found the candy. This earned her a trip to the vet, which she did not enjoy much at all. Then there was the Christmas poppy seed bread, given by a friend. I had a slice for breakfast one day and went to have one the next day as well. The bread was nowhere to be found. Three days later, we found the wrapper in the basement, where Chyna was known to go from time to time. It was a good thing she did not have to take a drug test.

   Chyna also became friends with our grand-dog, another Miles, the border collie mix. Miles would stay with us when they needed to be out of town, and it was great fun to watch Chyna and Miles run in the backyard. Chyna was the faster, due to her greyhound blood, but Miles was the more agile, so when he would begin to run, Chyna would chase and when she was about to catch him, he would suddenly turn, which Chyna could not do, so she would slide sideways trying to turn with him.

Chyna was loved by all our grandchildren, and she would gladly curl up on their laps when they would come to visit.

Not long after Mollies' death, our family grew again, when a friend asked if she could rehome her daughter's Boston Terrier, Olive, with us. Her daughter was on her way to college, Olive could not go with, and our friend was also unable to keep Olive. It took us about thirty seconds to agree. Olive's story will come later. Chyna met and grew to love Olive as she had Mollie.

After a time, we began to notice two things about Chyna. One, she was not moving as well, her hind legs seemingly unable to carry her well, with climbing stairs became more and more difficult. Arthritis was setting in, and she was slowing down appreciably. Then, more disturbing, she appeared at times, confused. She had begun to develop canine dementia. We were crushed. She was the same sweet Chyna, but she was not herself at the same time. When she could no longer go upstairs at all, when she could not even seem to understand things and would stand and stare, it became clear it was time.

Now Chyna normally hated going to the vet's office. When we would take her to the car and drive there, she would become aware of where she was and refuse to get out of the car. When she saw the building, she would lock legs as she had when we first met her and tried to put her back in the kennel. Again, it involved carrying her into the office, then into the exam room. It was exhausting, and she was no help in this.

The day the decision was made to let her go, it was like she was a different dog. She walked to the car, let me lift her into the backseat. At the vets parking lot she got out of the car on her own and walked across the lot to the office, walking in the door with no hesitation. When the tech called us back to the exam room, Chyna stood and walked between us into the room, looked around, and lay on the floor, where she stayed while the medication was administered, and with her head on my lap, she looked up, and I knew she knew. It was time. She was more ready then we were and crossed peacefully. We cried for days, and Olive and Rxby grieved openly, looking for the Chyna who was no longer there.

OLIVE

Olive came to us rather unexpectedly. We were sitting in bed one morning, cuddled with Myles, and Chyna when we received a phone call from a good friend asking if we could possibly take her daughter's dog, Olive, into our home. We were well acquainted with Olive, and it took us about thirty seconds to agree, even though we already had what we thought was our limit of dogs.

Olive had been the cancer-buddy for our friend's daughter, who had osteosarcoma. She was on her way to college, and Olive could not accompany her. Her mother had to move and could not take Olive with her to her new home either. Olive became the third dog in the household, no less loved than the others. Rxby became the fourth, more on him later.

Olive was, in many ways, the clone of Mollie, very similar in looks as well as in temperament. Boston Terriers both, they exemplified the breed as true companion dogs. She filled the space left by Mollie, and was accepted by the others immediately.

Olive was a quieter presence in the household and a constant reminder of our friend and her daughter. We never considered Olive ours; she was theirs, and we were given care of her for a season. Had they ever been able to take Olive back, we would have let her go with a blessing. Olive was part of their family before ours, and we counted it a privilege to care for this beautiful little Boston. It was, therefore, a harder decision when it became apparent that Olive was failing, and we only took her to be put to sleep after much discussion with our friend and her daughter, with their knowledge and consent.

Olive was the only dog whose ashes we have kept. For the others, we have paw print molds and have kept these with their collars. Olive we had the ashes returned to us and gave these to our friend's daughter. Olive was such a part of her young life that we could not refuse the ashes nor keep them ourselves. As Olive was with her in life, so should she be in death. It is my thought that when we all cross that bridge, Olive will acknowledge us only after she has run to another's arms.

RXBY

When we first met Rxby, we already had
three dogs in the family. We were on our way
to a neighborhood flea market/yard sale in one
of the old historic neighborhoods in our city.
Driving on a street on the near southeast side,
Cami became quite excited "did you see that?"
"What," I asked, "that scruffy little stray on the
sidewalk?" It turns out he was not just a "scruffy
little stray," it was a hairless Chinese Crested, not
a dog you would expect to find loose on a city
street.

We drove around the block and circled back,
looking for him. We spotted him in an alley
behind a warehouse. Getting out of the van, we
called him to us, and of course, he ran away. He
ended up in a fair-sized stand of trees and bushes
beside a concrete railroad trestle. He had made
a nest deep in the brush which included poison
ivy. With Cami going in on one end, I went to
the other, and we had him in between us. After

about 45 minutes, Cami managed to get hold of him without being bitten, which was her expectation. Little did we know he had very few teeth. As she was walking back to the van, he lay his head over and melted into her arms. That was the beginning of a bond to be broken only by his passing.

With the yard sale now off the agenda, we went straight to our vet's office to have this little guy scanned for a microchip. There was none. There was no collar, no tattoo, nothing to indicate who he had escaped from.   The vet thought he was about eight or nine years old but could not be sure due to the lack of teeth.

This little guy went home with us where we bathed him, took a picture, and tried every way we could think of to find his home, to no avail. The vet surmised that he might have been the pet of an elderly owner who died and, not wanting to care for him, the family turned him out to fend for himself, or he had simply run away. He had done remarkably well on his own when we found him.

Rxby, or Rex, as we named him, came into our home and pack. The first of our human family to meet him were my son and his two daughters. They had never seen a hairless breed before and weren't really too sure about petting him. That didn't last long. Rxby was well -trained. He had obviously been cared for in the past. He soon became an integral part of our household, accepted by and accepting the rest, making a place for himself in the pack and in our hearts. He soon became "Daddy's dog", seeming to like nothing more than crawling into my lap and having me stroke his skin. If I stopped petting him, he would paw at my hand to let me know he wanted more.

Rxby revealed himself as very intelligent. He showed us he could talk. When he wanted to go outside, he would stretch out his neck and bark at us in a very recognizable "OOWW," which sounded very much like "out." I would sometimes, not very nicely, tease him when he said that and encourage him to say it over and over before I let him out.

He was a planner. One time Cami was sitting on the floor playing with Olive when Rxby came by and made it clear he wanted Cami's attention, he wanted in her lap. He became quite insistent, pawing and barking almost under his breath at first, getting increasingly louder as his plea was ignored. Suddenly he stopped and just looked at the two of them then ran off into another room. Soon he returned with one of the Boston's favorite toys, stopped right in front of her, then ran off. Of course, she followed to get her toy. Before we knew it, Rxby was back, sitting in Cami's lap when the little Boston returned with her toy but without a lap to sit in.

Then there was the day I was home from work with a cold. I was resting on the sofa with my tea and toast when Rxby began to inform me he wanted to go out. There was the "OOWW", and he ran to the door and stood looking first at me then at the door. Obligingly I got up, went to the door and opened it, expecting to see Rxby run out only to find he was not there. Looking back, I caught sight of him, a slice of toast in his mouth, running off into the dining room. The little bugger had lured me away simply to steal my toast, which he managed to finish before I got to him.

Rxby was all boy, marking anything and everything he could, including my bare leg one day when I was washing the dishes and not paying him enough attention. He was the only male in our pack, which made him and me the lone men in a household of women. We would joke that the other girls were, in fact, Rxby's harem. He was quite protective of them, especially Coconut, a little Bichon Frise when she came to live with us. She is still with us.

We never knew his actual age, only that he was a senior. He began to fail and was diagnosed with Cushing's disease. We didn't kick in immediately to full hospice mode, because he didn't seem to be that in distress and because we have always leaned toward giving our little ones all the comfort we could regardless. He seemed to be doing all right, slowing down some but still the feisty yet cuddly little guy we found on the street. He was even able to go with us on our first trial run in our new "home on wheels, Burton's Ark" as we named our retirement home, a 36 ft class A motor home. We knew he would love traveling with us but were quite concerned that he might not live to do so. He did. We took a two-week trip that was supposed to be to Arizona by way of Louisiana and a visit with family. That trip was detoured back to Indianapolis due to some mechanical difficulties. Rxby was able to enjoy the two weeks on the road, the time in Louisiana with canine cousins Tibbe, a Shihtzu and Skipper, a Schnauzer. When back in Indianapolis he enjoyed a prolonged stay at an RV park while our house was on the market in preparation for full-time life on the road.

It was at that RV park where Rxby crashed, literally. He suddenly became very listless, his stool loose and bloody. He was just not himself. He would cuddle in my lap but ceased even to bark at other dogs and people when the girls did. We had him to an emergency vet who confirmed that the Cushings had progressed to pancreatitis, and medication was prescribed as a last-ditch effort. We knew that if it didn't turn around quickly, it would not. In short, it didn't. In less than two days, he showed more signs of discomfort with more blood in his stool. That was the turning point. This little boy who had introduced us to a breed we have come to love, this beautiful old soul should not and could not be allowed to suffer due to our not wanting to let go.

I remained back at the RV with the other girls, Mizani, Daphne, and Coconut, (all of whom are still with us)while Cami took Rxby back to the emergency vet to see if there was anything else that could be done. We knew that if there was not, or if it would only cause him more distress, we would not go there. It seemed, sadly, it was time to bid him farewell and let him have the rest he deserved. Cami came back home without him, and we cried. The two granddaughters who had been the first to meet him came to visit us that day, and we had a chance to talk to them about Rxby, whom they had grown to love, and why we made the decision, we did. He will ever be in my heart.

CODY

Yorkshire Terrier with cancer, hospice foster. Rehoming and essentially fostering Olive led us to consider fostering other dogs, particularly those of more advanced age or special needs, such as ill or injured dogs. This brought Cody into our home.

Codie was a cute little Yorkshire Terrier who had cancer of the mouth. While treatment was no longer an option for him, he was still able to eat and loved to wander. Rather than simply have him put down, the rescue organization approached us about fostering Cody as a hospice patient, leaving us also with the decision of when enough was enough for this brave little boy.

So Cody came into the pack. By then we had adopted three more, Mizani, Daphne and Coconut, who along with Rxby made up our pack. Cody blended well into our home. He was a quiet little fellow, never making much noise, but quietly wandering when he was not cuddled into one of our laps. He would take some time to settle in and be comfortable, but when he did, he was sound asleep.

   Cody had no objection to clothes, and some of our favorite photos of him are in a little plaid coat that did not fit any of our pack.

   Cody was with us only a couple of months when we noticed he was having a much more difficult time eating and was fussing with his mouth quite a bit. The cancer was getting much worse, and it was obvious that his pain and discomfort was growing. In consultation with the rescue, we took him to their vet, who agreed that letting him go would not be the wrong decision.

   So we took Cody and remained with him, as he was one of ours. We both held him, offering what comfort we could while the medication took effect; he closed his eyes and crossed the bridge. I hope to see him again, hold him, and let him fall asleep in my lap.

Cody came to us after Rxby and crossed the Rainbow Bridge before he did. Even though he was with us a short time, it seemed to us that all the others missed Cody when he was gone, as did we.

Miles

A Border collie mix, granddog.

During the writing of this memoir, Miles,
our border collie granddog crossed the rainbow
bridge. While Miles did not live in our home,
we cared for Miles often enough that we consider
him part of our pack.

Miles had been the "first child" of my son
and daughter-in-law, who didn't plan on having
children. Miles was a young rescue, energetic
as all border collies, and would come running to
the door when someone would come to the house
and leap at them.

Miles was used to sleeping at the foot of the
bed. When the baby came into the house, her
crib was there, and he simply moved a bit to give
her room. Then the crib was moved into the
nursery they had prepared, and Miles moved into

the nursery, taking his place sleeping at the foot of the crib. He had taken the new baby girl as his own, and through her infancy and toddler years, Miles was, true to his breed, her protector, herding the wandering child around the backyard, ever keeping her safe.

After another granddaughter was born, Miles had more work to do. When the girls would come to spend the night with us, Miles would always come with. Before they were born and we kept Miles, he would sleep on our bed with us and the rest of the pack. This changed when the girls were with us. Miles would take up a post in the doorway of the room in which they slept. His young charges were always safe whenever he was on duty.

There was one quirky thing about Miles. While he was a quiet dog, never barking, this all changed when he saw a man carrying a ladder. It didn't matter who the man was, a stranger or my son, any man carrying a ladder caused Miles to bark menacingly and move toward the man. He never harmed anyone, but this behavior remained a mystery until his dying day.

Miles crossed the rainbow bridge around age 15, and by that time another dog, Willis, a jack Russell-chihuahua mix had become part of the family. Willis was able to comfort the granddaughters, and their parents after Miles was gone.

Thus ends the list of those who, I sincerely hope, will be waiting at the other side of the bridge. I genuinely believe they are in heaven, and that heaven is indeed that place where all the dogs who have ever loved me or loved us will be there to greet us. What a beautiful place that will be. They will be at their best, and we will love each of them, telling them what a difference they have made in our lives, the lessons they taught us not always apparent at the time, coming to our awareness only later, sometimes much later.

These marvelous beings have souls, or rather their souls are part of that larger soul of which we are all a part, they just inhabit different bodies. They are no less precious in the sight of God, and at times I think they are truly the hands, feet, the voice and presence of God in our lives.

Contact the Author

For books and music and congenial conversation.

G.W. Burton contact info:
email: gordoburto@gmail.com

Books may be ordered through Glorybound Publishing at www.gloryboundpublishing.com and amazon.com.

About the Author
G.W. Burton

Gordon W. Burton was born in Oakland, California in 1951, moving with his parents to Indiana in 1953.

He spent his formative years in the little town of Brook, Indiana. After high school graduation in 1969, he spent a year in Germany as an exchange student.

Returning to Indiana, he attended and graduated from Indiana Central College in 1974, and Garrett-Evangelical Theological Seminary in 1977.

Gordon was a parish minister until 1983, when he moved to Indianapolis, Indiana to pursue a career as a staff chaplain at Methodist Hospital of Indiana. He served in that capacity for thirty years, retiring in 2017.

Upon retiring, Gordon and his wife Cami sold their house and moved into an RV with their four rescue dogs, Mizani, Daphne, Coconut, and Portia, and headed West, heeding the call of the red rocks of Sedona. After living for a time in the RV, they settled in the small town of Rimrock, Arizona, in the Verde Valley.

In addition to his writing, Gordon plays Native American flute at resorts in Sedona, Arizona, and at public and private events in Sedona and the greater Verde Valley area. Gordon has begun crafting Native American flutes out of Verde Valley bamboo.

Gordon and Cami enjoy travelling in the RV with their dogs, as well as hiking and kayaking and just hanging out with friends.

Made in United States
Orlando, FL
26 March 2024

45168491R00045